100

THINGS TO DO IN
BRANSON
BEFORE YOU
DIE

100

THINGS TO DO IN

BRANSON

BEFORE YOU

DIE

KAREN NELSON

REEDY PRESS

917.
7
N

Library of Congress Control Number: 2017964121

ISBN: 9781681061382

Design by Jill Halpin

Printed in the United States of America
18 19 20 21 22   5 4 3 2 1

Please note that websites, phone numbers, addresses, and company names are subject to change or cancellation. We did our best to relay the most accurate information available, but due to circumstances beyond our control, please do not hold us liable for misinformation. When exploring new destinations, please do your homework before you go.

DEDICATION

This book is dedicated to Fred and Faye Pfister, my "favorite" uncle and aunt, for their outstanding representation of what it means to be part of a community that supports the arts and education. They have long been champions of the Ozarks and the Branson area, delighting in the quirky, applauding progress, and preserving the heritage of this beautiful region. To me, they *are* Branson. A cushioned chair is waiting, something simmers on the stove, and the door is always open.

CONTENTS

● ●

• •

• •

Culture and History

• •

Shopping and Fashion

PREFACE

Straddling two counties and three lakes, Branson and the surrounding area is a world of its own. Driving into the Ozark Mountains is like settling into Granny's embrace—the hills are a little stooped with age, and she shows her wrinkles in the rock outcroppings, but you know there is a deeper wisdom here than you can fathom. You are connected to something older than yourself. You feel safe and discover a richness that can't be found in the stock market or a bank.

It's a richness that stretches back to the Osage Indians, who knew every bent tree and curve of the White River here. When settlers arrived in the 1800s, they found peace and a sense of belonging among the oaks and pines and trickling streams. Attracted by the innovative talents of the Herschend family and Harold Bell Wright and his book *The Shepherd of the Hills*, tourists arrived in the early 1900s to explore the natural beauty of the hills and plumb the depths of Marvel Cave. The 1960s brought the Beverly Hillbillies to life, straight from the Ozark Mountains—you can see their dilapidated car piled high with possessions at the Ralph Foster Museum.

And then there's the music. Roy Clark, Boxcar Willie, Andy Williams, Glen Campbell, the Oak Ridge Boys, Ray Stevens, Mickey Gilley, Tony Orlando, Mel Tillis, and Bobby Vinton have all had permanent theater shows on the famous "Strip." The town has sparked the careers of Shoji Tabuchi, the Presleys, the Baldknobbers, and more, with visits from Loretta Lynn, Conway Twitty, Waylon Jennings, Don Williams, Charley Pride, and other non-country artists, such as REO Speedwagon, Lynyrd Skynyrd,

• •

and Def Leppard. The list goes on, and so does the artistic talent of current entertainers who offer everything from comedy to acrobatics. (More about that in the pages ahead.)

Of course, there is more than shows. There's golfing and hiking and go-karting and bargain-hunting and boating and fishing and dining and fireworks . . . and lots of things I haven't tried yet, even after twenty-five years as a resident.

As time has passed, I've come to appreciate how diverse my home truly is. Once a music mecca, Branson now hosts endless opportunities for outdoor adventures, historical encounters, and shopping excursions. A scenic drive delights in any season, with vast panoramic views from the tops of mountain ridgelines. You can take in the filming sites for movies such as *Gordy* and *Winter's Bone*. There isn't a day I drive through town that I don't notice something new popping up.

For me, Branson isn't just about the past or losing yourself in a weekend's play. It's about finding what you love—a trail to a waterfall (Lakeside Forest Wilderness Area), a new instrument to play (Cedar Creek Dulcimers), a hobby with friends (Scrapbooks Forever), or that one roadside stop that never lets you down (Danna's BBQ). Branson never disappoints because it is rooted in something more than mere entertainment.

• •

Coming here twenty-five years ago felt like coming home to Granny's. I can see why she stayed—why I stayed—and why you will, too.

A WORD ABOUT THE STRIP

Highway 76, MO-76, 76 Country Boulevard, US Highway 76, "the Strip"...there are multiple names for the same winding road that bisects Branson. This is the main thoroughfare for the town, and it is lined with the bulk of Branson's theaters, museums, and attractions.

While the details of the listed physical address may change from one location to the next, they all refer to the same Highway 76, so if you see multiple street names on your GPS list with "76" in them, they refer to the same road.

If you are using GPS to locate area attractions, Branson has only one ZIP code—65616.

• •

FOOD AND DRINK

GET STUFFED
AT KIM'S BBQ SHACK

My family needs a BBQ fix at least once a week, and this is the only place we consider. A former Danna's BBQ (with multiple Branson locations), Kim's is under new ownership but serves the same delicious food. The pulled pork, giant hamburgers, and monster-size salads are mere sidekicks to the star spuds at these local restaurants. Baked potatoes the size of a small shovel are stuffed with pulled pork (or chicken or beef), baked beans, butter, sour cream, and cheese and are topped with bacon. For a buttery treat, take a six-pack of Memphis rolls with you for later.

Stick a fork in me. I'm done.

Kim's BBQ Shack
7930 E. Hwy. 76, Branson
417-334-9541

Danna's BBQ
963 State Hwy. 165, Branson
417-337-5527

Danna's BBQ
15 Hope Way, Reeds Spring
417-272-1945
dannasbbq.com

GET SERVICE WITH A SONG
AT MEL'S HARD LUCK DINER

Branson was founded on music, so why not have some with your fries? The singing servers at Mel's Hard Luck Diner will have you groovin' and smilin' to their tunes, as well as to the Sixteen Ton Chili Burger. The fifties decor and soda fountain rock around the clock. You can't help but be happy when you walk through the door.

The menu is packed with mouthwatering choices, but be sure you read all the way to the bottom 'cause you are going to want the crowning dessert . . . the Climb Every Mountain Ice Cream Avalanche: *twelve* scoops of ice cream topped with cookies, brownie crumbles, bananas, pineapple, strawberries, hot fudge, caramel, marshmallow cream, and M&Ms. The diner calls it "family-sized."

2800 W. 76 Country Blvd., Suite 103, Branson
417-332-0150
melshardluckdiner.com

JOIN THE ROUNDUP
AT THE CHUCKWAGON DINNER SHOW

The smell of smoked barbeque and the sight of red checkered tablecloths are the first clues that this is going to be a great dinner. You'll feel right at home on the range with the friendly atmosphere and treats from the trail. (The pulled pork and roasted ears of corn are a personal favorite.)

Enjoy the flavors of the Wild West with the musicians of New Trails, playing classics of country and Western swing. You can scoot your boot or simply feast on the brisket, home-fried taters, and corn. Folks love the real chuckwagon and cowboy feel and get a bang out of the cowboy poetry.

Don't worry about getting a good seat for the show—this venue has an around-the-campfire feel that makes any spot a good one to hear the sweet harmonies of those cowpoke crooners. You will, however, want to bring a warm coat or blanket during cooler evenings, as it can get chilly after the sun goes down. Grab a pardner and head to the roundup!

5586 W. Hwy. 76, Branson
417-334-4191
rounduponthetrail.com

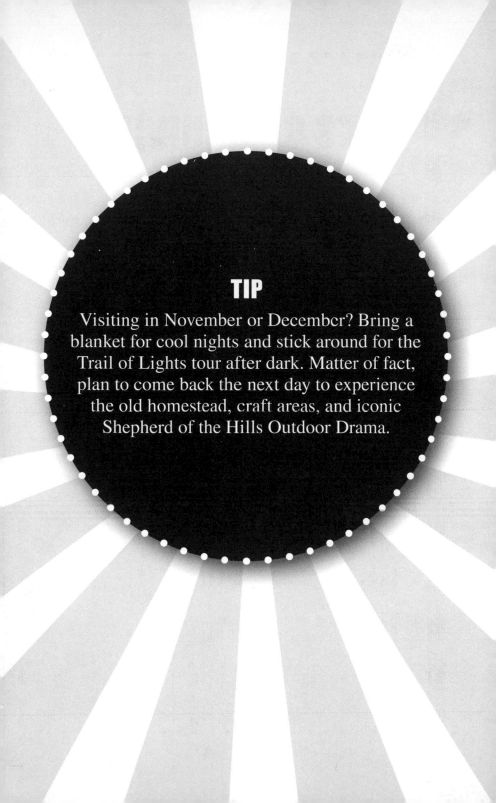

TIP

Visiting in November or December? Bring a blanket for cool nights and stick around for the Trail of Lights tour after dark. Matter of fact, plan to come back the next day to experience the old homestead, craft areas, and iconic Shepherd of the Hills Outdoor Drama.

LET'S DO BRUNCH

Nothing makes me feel more spoiled than going out for brunch at the Keeter Center or Top of the Rock. I've been trying to decide which has the best Sunday-only selections, but it's still a toss-up. On the one hand, College of the Ozarks' Keeter Center offers farm-to-table variety served by international students in the culinary program (and you can spend the afternoon exploring the mill, greenhouses, and grounds). On the other hand, Top of the Rock has champagne and gourmet dishes I can't pronounce, and I can feel like I'm a socialite from the 1920s in the historic buildings.

I'm looking forward to years of "market research" as I continue to compare the best brunch options in Branson, but you really can't go wrong with either of these two premier establishments. You can usually get in around 10 a.m., but any later and you'll want reservations. Don't sleep in too late, because they close up after noon, and you are going to want at least two hours to take it all in. Oh, and be sure to wear elastic-waist pants. Just trust me on that one.

College of the Ozarks, Keeter Center
1 Opportunity Ave., Point Lookout
417-690-2146, keetercenter.edu

Osage Restaurant, Top of the Rock
190 Top of the Rock Rd., Ridgedale
417-335-2777
topoftherock.com/dining/osage-restaurant-en.html

FIND CENTER-STAGE NIGHTLIFE
AT BACKSTAGE WINE BAR

It would be easy to miss this oasis in downtown Branson, but you'd be sorry. Housed in one of the original Branson structures and the 1903 Branson Hotel, Backstage Wine Bar is *the* place to sample wines from around the world and hear musicians from around the area. The indoor bar is gorgeous, with wood paneling and decor that feels like you've stepped into a European winery. In fact, the entire property reflects the love and care its world-traveling owners have put into it. The hidden gem of this venue is the intimate, enclosed back garden with a fire pit and generous seating. You'd never guess you were in the heart of a bustling tourist town!

It's open until 11 p.m., so you can get in on happy hour (4 p.m. to 6 p.m.) or stop in after a show for an evening glass. There is no parking on the street, so circle the block for spaces at nearby businesses, or park behind the hotel.

214 W. Main St., Branson
417-334-8550
backstagecafeandwinebar.com

OOH-LA-LATTE
AT VINTAGE PARIS COFFEE AND WINE CAFÉ

Vintage Paris is one of those places you wish you had in your neighborhood. The house is a hundred years old, but the vibe is all now. Whether you are snug in a corner sipping a loose-leaf tea, chatting with friends over one of the café's in-house roasted coffees, or sampling a craft beer by the fire pit on the patio, this local gem will be a welcome break in your adventures. It's become a bit of a local secret, and you can sometimes find local musicans playing there on warm summer evenings. It's even been the site of the Taneycomo Festival Orchestra performances in June. You'll feel like you've been whisked away to a Paris café!

Be sure to call ahead for evening music events, and take note of the local art on display.

260 Birdcage Walk, Hollister
417-593-7952
vintagepariscoffeeshop.com

TIP

Don't miss the entire historic Downing Street in Hollister. Wander north from Vintage Paris and peruse the antique shops, peek at Ye Olde English Inn, and check out the original train depot.

TASTE THE OZARKS
AT A LOCAL WINERY

Missouri vineyards have been winning awards for their vintages for decades, and there is no better place to sample them all in one place than in Branson. Each location is unique, not to mention delicious!

Curling Vine Winery, an offshoot of Stone Hill Winery, has a free tour that ends with a sampling of its extensive collection. All ages enjoy watching the historical video and the bottling process, and even kids can join in the tasting with some of the sparkling juices.

Lindwedel Winery sits atop a hill overlooking the mountains, and visitors can sample their favorite red and white wines from the winery's gorgeous garden. Lindwedel also offers a unique wine club program and has Sunday afternoon music events in the fall, as well as other events year-round.

St. James Winery Branson is the newest addition to the Branson wine tour, with a fabulous lunch and dinner menu. In the heart of Branson, visitors can sample several selections (my favorites are the blackberry and peach wines!), then get a table near the brick alcoves and order the antipasto platter while looking over the delectable menu.

Curling Vine Winery
Highway 165 and Green Mountain Drive, Branson
417-334-1897
curlingvinewinery.com

Lindwedel Winery
3158 Hwy. 265, Branson
417-338-0256
lindwedelwinery.com

St. James Winery Branson
405 State Hwy. 165, Branson
417 544 8283
stjameswinery.com/find-us-in-branson

HAVE SOME DOWN-UNDER FUN
AT OUTBACK STEAK AND OYSTER BAR

The Outback (no relation to the restaurant chain) has been the talk of Branson since it arrived on the Strip and treated locals to baked snapper and alligator tail. The Australian-themed restaurant serves unique dishes and drinks, but the real attraction is the chance to relax Aussie-style. There's something about the expansive decks, fire pit, decor, and landscaping that invites you to leave your cares behind and have a g'day, mate!

If you stop in at happy hour at the Outback Pub next door, you'll be entertained by local musicians, and there's a DJ on the party deck every Friday and Saturday night. For those who love the laidback life, there's no greater place than down under.

1914 W. 76 Country Blvd., Branson
417-334-6306
outbackbranson.com

GET THE BEST BURGER IN TOWN
AT BILLY BOB'S DAIRYLAND

When I was a kid, there was a little hole-in-the-wall restaurant that served enormous juicy cheeseburgers that still make my mouth water just thinking about them. Walking into Billy Bob's feels like I've gone back home and become a kid again. This is the classic diner experience—burgers made to order, fries, shakes, and fried pies.

You could read the rave reviews online or just check the parking lot (it's always packed) to know how good the place is. There can be a bit of a wait, but you can usually get in just before five o'clock. It's a cash-only kind of place, so keep that in mind before you head over. Heck, just go to the ATM, because you're going to be back for more.

1829 W. 76 Country Blvd., Branson
417-337-9291

GET ON A (CINNAMON) ROLL
AT GRANDMA RUTH'S

Ever wish you could step back in time to your grandma's kitchen, watch her roll out dough and then look up and smile, and know it was just for you? Well, Grandma Ruth is everybody's grandma, and she's still at it, serving up plate hangers (that's rolls so big they hang over the edges of the plate). You can smell the icing before you get through the door, and just when you think you're going to get a standard cinnamon roll—which is still out of this world— you realize Grandma Ruth makes caramel, toffee, a special flavor of the week, and sugar cookies. Other menu items are available, depending on what day of the week you stop in, and Friday and Saturday mornings from 8:30 to 11 a.m., the incredible John Fullerton sings cowboy classics such as "Ghost Riders in the Sky" and "Tumbling Tumbleweeds."

9 Treasure Lake Rd., Branson
417-231-5900
grandmaruths.net

GET CREAMED
AT ANDY'S FROZEN CUSTARD

The after-show treat . . . don't leave Branson without visiting this Missouri original (now the largest dessert-only franchise in the world!). It seems like all of Branson can be found here after the shows let out. There always seems to be a line at the walk-up window and a line of cars through the drive-through. Maybe it's the bright lights and 1950s aesthetic, or the sock-hoppin' music played outside, but this place is plumb irresistible.

You just haven't had ice cream until you've had a creamy frozen custard, and Andy's is the best by far. Whether you are a plain vanilla person or a chocoholic, Andy's has a flavor to suit your fancy. My family loves the old-fashioned sugar cones, but I prefer mine in a cup. A waffle cone might be just the ticket, or you could go for a sample size—arguably the cutest miniature cone ever invented.

What's the difference between ice cream and frozen custard? Custard is slow-churned cream with more butterfat, for starters. The brownies, caramel, and seasonal flavors just add to the experience. I'd love to recommend a few things on the menu, but, honestly, I can't get past the Ozark Turtle. Start with Andy's signature vanilla custard and top with caramel, chocolate, and peanuts. It's calling me even now.

3415 W. 76 Country Blvd., Branson
417-337-5501, eatandys.com

TICKLE YOUR TASTE BUDS
AT THE BELGIAN WAFFLE AND PANCAKE HOUSE

Breakfast is a blast from the past at this timeless American diner serving classic, lighter-than-air waffles. Get yours with cinnamon and sugar, fruit topping, or pecans and whipped cream. Of course, the other breakfast platters will get you fueled up for your day of fun. And the lunch menu has mouthwatering fillers such as the One-Half Pound Hamburger and the Triple Threat Club Sandwich.

The real attraction (besides the waffles) is the friendly service from the staff—some of whom are still serving up happiness going on twenty years. Ask for one of Rhonda's tables, and she'll make sure you get treated right. It's a Branson institution!

3120 W. 76 Country Blvd., Branson
417-334-8484
belgianwaffleandpancake.com

Lines too long for the Belgian Waffle House?
You can still get breakfast at several nearby restaurants.

IHOP
1055 W. Hwy. 376, Branson
417-339-4467
ihop.com

Clockers Café
103 S. Commercial St., Branson
417-335-2328
clockerscafe.com

Farmhouse Restaurant
119 W. Main St. S., Branson
417-334-9701
farmhouserestaurantbranson.com

Grand Country Buffet
1945 W. 76 Country Blvd., Branson
417-335-2434
grandcountry.com/restaurants

McFarlain's Family Restaurant
3562 Shepherd of the Hills Expy., Branson
417-336-4680
bransonimax.com/dining

WET YOUR WHISTLE
AT WAXY O'SHEA'S IRISH PUB

Waxy O'Shea's is my happy place. From the wood paneling and snug seating to the live music and trivia nights, I feel like I'm back in Ireland again. This little slice of Dublin is perfectly situated in the heart of the Branson Landing, which means you can tuck into the pub fare between shops or while away an afternoon sampling the largest selection of draft beers in town. It even runs in true Irish style and offers *two* happy hours every day.

I'm a sucker for shepherd's pie and fish and chips, but you might want to try the boxty, in four varieties, or the Guinness pot roast for a real taste of the Emerald Isle. And on a cold day, nip in for a Bailey's hot chocolate. You'll never want to go home again.

235 Branson Landing, Branson
417-348-1759
waxyosheas.com

TIP

Most evenings Thursday through Saturday, you'll be treated to live entertainment starting at 9 p.m. It's a great end to a day at the Landing!

BUTTER UP
AT LAMBERT'S CAFÉ

"Hot rolls!"

That's what you'll hear seconds before one sails by your head. Get your catcher's stance ready, because these bread balls get pitched clear across the room. At Lambert's Café, home of the throwed rolls, diners get treated to "pass-arounds" (fried taters, stewed tomatoes, black-eyed peas, fried okra, and, of course, the homemade rolls) even before they lay eyes on the ginormous meal they've ordered.

Lambert's is an experience all in itself. It doesn't take reservations, but the wait is definitely worth it. Technically, the family-owned icon isn't in Branson . . . it's in Ozark, about twenty minutes north. But that's no reason not to start your vacation early or extend it on the way home. As my dad says, "If you leave hungry, it's your own fault!"

1800 W. State Hwy. J, Ozark
417-581-7655
throwedrolls.com

WANNA HURTS DONUT?

There are only three things you need to know:

1) Maple-bacon glaze is only the beginning.
2) There are swings in the front window instead of seats.
3) Just say yes.

1580 W. Hwy. 76, Branson
417-598-3474
facebook.com/Hurts-Donut-Branson-Missouri-1846285758938404/

Sweet tooth still need a fix? Try these other delicious doughnut eateries in the area:

Krispy Kreme
150 Tanger Blvd., Branson
417-339-2664
krispykreme.com

Dunkin' Donuts
1305 Hwy. 76, Branson
417-334-4099
dunkindonuts.com

Grandma Ruth's Old-Fashioned Cinnamon Rolls
9 Treasure Lake Rd., Branson
417-231-5900
grandmaruths.net

Yummy Donuts
15735 Hwy. 160, Forsyth
417-546-8993

PICK AN OZARK PRIZE
AT A BERRY FARM

If you were lucky enough to go berry picking as a kid, you probably remember the scratches, chiggers, and mosquitoes, not to mention fighting birds and bugs to get a pailful of purple fruit for a pie. Now imagine tidy mulched rows with nary a pest in sight, where clusters of plump berries almost leap into your hand. That's what awaits you at Persimmon Hill (blueberries and mushrooms) and Blackberry Lane (blackberries, raspberries, and grapes).

This is old-fashioned fun with a purpose. Not only do you go home with the fruits of your labor, but you can also treat yourself to some of their on-site goodies. Persimmon Hill specializes in Thunder Muffins and blueberry pancakes, shakes, and syrups. Blackberry Lane offers up hand-cranked homemade ice cream and blackberry cobbler. The farms are located on opposite sides of Branson and are open seasonally, so call ahead to make sure the time is ripe for your visit.

Blackberry Lane Farm
732 State Hwy. O, Kissee Mills
417-546-4939
facebook.com/BlackberryLaneFarms

Persimmon Hill Farm
367 Persimmon Hill Ln., Lampe
417-779-5443
persimmonhill.com

HAVE A FLOATING DINNER
AT WHITE RIVER FISH HOUSE

This is a Bass Pro property, so you know it has rustic charm and outdoor flair. Besides the novelty of gator nuggets and sweet jalapeño cornbread, there is a staggering variety of fish dishes . . . all at a window seat on the water. And we mean water—the whole restaurant is floating on Lake Taneycomo!

If the weather is fine, snag a patio seat and watch the boats and kayaks drift by with the ducks. You might even catch sight of a blue heron along the bank.

Park at the south end of the Branson Landing and walk across the gangplank for a uniquely vintage experience. It's the perfect end (or beginning!) to an evening at the Landing.

1 Bass Pro Dr., Branson
417-243-5100
restaurants.basspro.com/whiteriverfishhouse

MAKE A MOONSHINE RUN
AT A LOCAL DISTILLERY

Moonshine, rotgut, hillbilly pop, bathtub gin, white lightning, firewater, sugar whiskey, mule kick, ruckus juice, mountain dew . . . whatever you call it, this hooch with a history is being served up in new flavors (but with the same old Mason jars).

Copper Run is the first legal moonshine distillery in the Ozark Mountains since 1933, when Prohibition ended. It prides itself on being a small craft distillery; you can learn more about it through its Signature Barrel program. If you're looking for local, this is it. Copper Run uses local resources, such as the limestone-rich Missouri water, and white oak barrels. Its White Whiskey and Corn Whisky are both award-winning releases—and you can enjoy a free sample in the tasting rooms.

Smith Creek Distillery boasts flavors from Tennessee to the Branson Landing, with its charming mountain culture decor, hamburger restaurant, and souvenir sets with bottled shines, sauces, and more. Shine lovers will be impressed by the unique flavors, including salted caramel, sweet tea, apple pie, and gingersnap. Free sips can be had at the tasting bar in the shop.

TIP

Check out the schedule online for
Copper Run's live music offerings!

Copper Run Distillery and Tasting Room
1901 Day Rd., Walnut Shade
417-587-3456
copperrundistillery.com

Smith Creek Distillery
1209 Branson Landing Blvd., Branson
800-441-5053
smithcreekmoonshine.com

SEE THE SUNSET
AT TOP OF THE ROCK

The Top of the Rock has a lot to offer since its development by Bass Pro owner Johnny Morris. Outdoor sporting, wilderness trails, and a cave tour are just a sampling of the rustic-themed options south of Branson. But this is more than crossbows and canoes. Top of the Rock is the premier location for an elegant evening out. Guests rave about the sunset scenes from the signature Osage Restaurant.

The views are spectacular, the food superb. The Osage Restaurant is where you want to go for a special night out. Make a reservation, put on a collared shirt, and splurge on the bison fondue appetizer. The menu may be pricey, but the romance is complimentary!

Top of the Rock
190 Top of the Rock Rd., Ridgedale
417-335-2777
topoftherock.com

TIP

All cars are charged a ten-dollar fee to enter the property, but this is credited toward any purchase or admission to the cave or golf course.

For a more relaxed meal (and pocketbook) with the same beautiful lodge decor and scenery, try some of the other dining options at the Top of the Rock preserve, such as Arnie's Barn, the Buffalo Bar, the "End of the Trail" All-American Wine Cellar, or Big Cedar Lodge.

MUSIC AND ENTERTAINMENT

GET THE BIG PICTURE
WITH THESE GIANT PHOTO OPS

You know you want to . . . get out that selfie stick and take some of the goofiest pictures to be found in the country. Branson embraces the larger-than-life, and you can too at these (free!) roadside attractions. Climb into the giant rocking chair, get your air guitar on in front of the massive fiddle and banjo at Grand Country, play with perspective by the giant meatball at Pasghetti's Italian Restaurant, and pose between the legs of the bizarrely oversized chicken at the Great American Steak and Chicken House. You'll find these and more up and down "the Strip"—Highway 76 Country Boulevard.

Branson RV Sales and Service
(giant JFK head)
5717 Hwy. 165, Branson

Grand Country Resort
(giant fiddle and guitar)
1945 W. 76 Country Blvd., Branson

Grand Village Shops
(giant rocking chair)
2800 Hwy. 76, Branson

Great American Steak and Chicken House
(giant chicken)
2421 W. 76 Country Blvd., Branson

Hollywood Wax Museum
(Giant castle, Mt. Rushmore, Kong King . . .
it's copyrighted, just go with it.)
3030 W. 76 Country Blvd., Unit A, Branson

Pasghetti's Italian Restaurant
(giant meatball)
3129 W. State Hwy. 76, Branson
(Try the indoor Ferris wheel, too!)

Promised Land Zoo
(giant gorilla)
2751 Shepherd of the Hills Expy., Branson

Ripley's Believe It or Not!
(giant Transformer Optimus Prime)
3326 W. Hwy. 76, Branson

T-Shirt Shack
(giant Ronald Reagan head)
3430 W. 76 Country Blvd., Branson
(Both Ronnie and JFK were brought here when South
Dakota's Presidents Park closed. They are made of concrete
and steel, and each weighs about ten thousand pounds!)

SEE FIRE AND WATER UNITE
AT THE BRANSON LANDING FOUNTAIN SHOW

It's fun, free, and fabulous. Catch this hourly show anytime between noon and 10 p.m. at Branson Landing's Town Square. The $7.5 million display of water, fire, light, and music is a spectacular sight—even in daylight. My favorite is to grab a table on the patio overlooking Lake Taneycomo at Cantina Laredo. Best seats in the house! (But you can also view the show from the amphitheater and steps leading down to the 1.5-mile boardwalk along the water. Or, catch a lake cruise tour and see the show from the other side!)

100 Branson Landing Blvd., Branson
bransonlanding.com

TAKE A SPIN!
AT THE TRACK

You could probably try a different go-kart track every day of the week in Branson and still have some to spare. By far, the Track Family Fun Parks have the most to choose from, including the wooden track at Wild Woody, the Lumberjack, Heavy Metal High Rise, and special pee-wee courses for the little ones. Each Track location works cooperatively with the other locations. (They even have a handy map to help you get around the many attractions.) Most offer combo passes to cover rides, arcade games, putt-putt, and a host of other entertainments. Buckle up and let's ride!

Mountain Ridge Racer Indoor Go-Karts
Grand Country Resort
1945 W. 76 Country Blvd., Branson
888-514-1088
grandcountry.com

The Track Family Fun Parks
3345 W. 76, Branson
417-334-1612
bransontracks.com

Xtreme Racing Center of Branson
3600 W. Hwy. 76, Branson
888-972-9958
xtremeracingcenterbranson.com

GET TWISTED UP
AT ACROBATS OF CHINA THEATRE

I don't think there's another show in Branson that takes my breath away quite like the Acrobats of China. Their unbelievable feats of strength, balance, and flexibility reflect their professional skills as athletes and artists. Some cast members go on to train for the Olympics. Seeing one of their shows is like taking a trip to the other side of the world, complete with beautiful sets, eye-catching colors, and brilliant costumes.

Unlike other shows, the Acrobats showcase their country's history and traditions in routines such as hoop diving, jar juggling, spinning plates, flipping bowls, and the chair stack. I confess, I spent a large part of the show holding my breath. But these consummate performers (some as young as six!) know how to entertain and delight.

BE A SINGING SENSATION
AT KARAOKE NIGHT

Whether you like the everybody-knows-your-name atmosphere (Bucketlist) or the funky eclectic hangout of the entertainers (Steampunk Pub and Grill), there's a place for you and your favorite song in Branson. I may be biased, but I happen to think Branson has more than the average amount of talent in town. Lots of locals come out to take the mic, and you'll frequently find some professional entertainers cutting loose after hours with songs you won't hear in the shows. Karaoke night varies for each establishment, so call ahead for starting times. And don't be bashful . . . if you're going to sing anywhere other than the shower, this is the best city to make your debut!

Beverly's Steakhouse and Saloon
1482 E. Hwy. 76, Branson
417-334-6508

Coulee's Bar and Grill
5378 State Hwy. 256, Branson
417-320-6029, couleesbarandgrill.com

Steampunk Pub and Grill
3307 W. 76 Country Blvd., Branson
417-239-1505

Bucketlist
4580 N. Gretna Rd., Branson
417-320-6216, facebook.com/bucketlistbranson

SEE A SHOW UNDER THE STARS
AT SHEPHERD OF THE HILLS
OUTDOOR DRAMA

The inspiration for the beginning of tourism in the Ozarks unfolds before your eyes in this expansive amphitheater. You'll follow Harold Bell Wright's original story of Ol' Matt, Aunt Mollie, Young Matt, and Sammy Lane. It's something of an Ozark *Romeo and Juliet* with some plot twists and surprising revelations. My family still thrills when they feel the heat from the cabin fire scene (yes, real fire) and the thundering of actors arriving on horseback. For a bit of fun during the intermission, head down to the stage and join the hoedown.

There's something magical about having a mountain sunset as the backdrop to this story of young love and gunfights, with horses racing and a log cabin ablaze. It truly is an essential experience for understanding Ozark heritage (and what a baldknobber really is!).

5586 W. Hwy. 76, Branson
417-334-4191
theshepherdofthehills.com

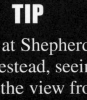

TIP

Make a day of it at Shepherd of the Hills
by touring the homestead, seeing craftspeople
at work, taking in the view from Inspiration
Tower, and ziplining down to a Chuckwagon
Supper before the show. It's old-fashioned
family fun you won't soon forget!

CARVE OUT TIME FOR ART
AT TITANIC'S ANNUAL WOODCARVING COMPETITION

Who knew that a chainsaw and a stick of wood could come together as a delicate work of art? Each year Titanic Branson, in association with LogHoggers Chainsaw Sculpting, hosts a competition where you can see just that. Images and sculptures are created on site before these one-of-a-kind works are auctioned to the highest bidders. It's a fascinating look at an unusual art, and the sculptures make for great conversation pieces in your own landscaping. You may even see some of past years' projects on display around town.

Call ahead for specific dates (and plan to go through the *Titanic* museum itself) and learn all the ways to split, slice, chip, and carve your way to appreciating this old German pastime.

3235 W. 76 Country Blvd., Branson
800-381-7670
titanicbranson.com

MAKE LEGENDARY MEMORIES
AT LEGENDS IN CONCERT

When Elvis left the building, he went to Branson. So have Adele, David Bowie, Johnny Cash, Dolly Parton, Liberace, Michael Jackson, Neil Diamond, and a host of other legendary entertainers. These live tribute shows seem kitschy from the billboards, but they are actually quite good fun. Talented singers and musicians have cultivated the essence of our favorite artists. The marquee has a constant rotation of stars that you can see for a fraction of the price in Las Vegas, Myrtle Beach, or Waikiki. And while you're there, check out the legendary movie cars parked next door.

Dick Clark's American Bandstand Theater
1600 W. Hwy. 76, Branson
417-339-3003
legendsinconcert.com

GET SPIT AT BY A LLAMA
AT SIGHT AND SOUND THEATRES

Okay, to be fair, the llama was backstage, and I was a little too close with a noisy child. Somehow, I was still charmed. Mostly because Sight and Sound Theatres is a thrill for the senses. With its eyepopping sets and costumes, dramatic story themes, and vocal talent sure to raise goosebumps, this show is an annual favorite for locals and visitors alike. Each production focuses on a biblical character and brings his or her story to life in a full Broadway-style production. The best-kept secret about this impeccably professional show is its backstage tours . . . for *free*! See the sets up close, get a chuckle out of just how many helmets and swords line the shelves, and meet some of the live animals that take the stage every night. You might even meet the llama. You'll need to call ahead for the schedule and to reserve your spot, but it is definitely worth the stop—and the price of admission.

1001 Shepherd of the Hills Expy., Branson
800-377-1277
sight-sound.com

PLAN YOUR ESCAPE
AT ESCAPE CODE

Escape rooms are all the rage, with participants puzzling their way out of "locked" rooms with a series of clues and settings. This is one activity that is engaging for the whole family, but it features levels to make it more challenging for some. This is our go-to place for rainy afternoon fun away from a screen. There are several locations in Branson, so you can try multiple scenarios, but call ahead to reserve a time and let them know how many people are in your party. We've found that four is a good number. Any less, and you may be put with other players (which is a fun way to meet people, but if you are on your own, it may be tough to solve in time).

Escape Code
4560 Gretna Rd., Branson
417-365-7999
escapecode.tv

Cryptex Escape Games
1819 W. 76 Country Blvd., Branson
417-320-6263
cryptexbranson.com

The Escape Branson
203 S. Commercial St., Branson
417-334-6620
theescapebranson.com

MAKE A REQUEST
AT ERNIE BIGGS DUELING PIANO BAR

Non-smoking, twenty-one and up only, and the music starts at 8 p.m. This entertaining bar with a concert-like atmosphere makes for a fun evening with friends. Whether you sit at the band-side bar or kick back at a table, the music will have you on your feet before the night is out. Often, three players rotate on two pianos, showcasing multiple abilities on drums, keyboard, and vocals. The talent is constantly changing, so plan on going back for more than one night. Can't spare an evening? Go anyway! The musicians may be on break during the day, but the food and service are always a treat.

505 Branson Landing Blvd., Branson
417-239-3670
erniebiggs.com/branson

GET IN ON THE HORSEPLAY
AT DIXIE STAMPEDE

Dixie Stampede is an annual pilgrimage for my family. I honestly can't pick one best thing about this experience. From the lasso tricks in the Carriage House before the show to the delicious cream of vegetable soup that starts off a mouthwatering meal, I feel like I've already had a good time before the actual entertainment even starts! Then come the horses, flame rings, musical numbers, ostrich antics, racing piglets, and good-natured rivalry from time gone by. Because the food keeps on coming, your hands are usually full, so if you see something you like . . . stampede! The arena is made for kickin' and stompin', so let loose and join the fun.

1525 W. 76 Country Blvd., Branson
877-782-6733
dixiestampede.com

SEE THE BIG SCREEN
AT BRANSON IMAX
ENTERTAINMENT COMPLEX

IMAX theaters have popped up around the world, but I never get tired of seeing the local city's special feature. Hollywood blockbusters and educational films rotate through the schedule, but one film is always available in Branson—*Ozarks: Legacy and Legend*. This is a wonderful introduction to the area's history, with local actors and nearby locations to help you feel connected to the region. Travel through time from the first settlers to the Branson boom, soaking in the scenery and sampling the mountain music that has made us what we are today. It's a great stop for first-timers to the Ozarks, but if you've missed it on earlier trips, make it a priority this time.

3562 Shepherd of the Hills Expy., Branson
417-335-4832
bransonimax.com

TIP

There's more to IMAX than movies . . . plan
to eat at McFarlain's Restaurant (the cornbread
makes the angels sing), shop the boutiques
indoors, and catch a live comedy or tribute
show at the Little Opry Theatre adjacent
to the big screen. My personal favorite?
The Sons of Britches!

HONK A WACKY QUACKER
ON RIDE THE DUCKS

Any town worth its salt will offer a city tour, but it isn't often you get a tour of the lake, too! These World War II amphibious vehicles, with their fun-loving paint jobs and joke-cracking drivers, will whisk you through the sights of Branson. But hold on tight: you're about to splash down in the waters of our beautiful lakes. No worries! You aren't likely to get wet. Don't miss the chance to "drive" the boat along the shore, and be sure to pick up a Wacky Quacker on your way through the museum and gift shop back at the depot. It's a unique souvenir from a truly memorable tour.

2320 W. Hwy. 76, Branson
877-887-8255
branson.ridetheducks.com

THANK YOUR DENTIST
AT THE PRESLEYS' AND
BALDKNOBBER SHOWS

The cartoon version of an Ozark hillbilly includes ragged overalls, a patched-up floppy hat, and a less-than-full set of teeth ... or none at all! You'll get the picture from the billboards as you drive into town, but give the entertainers a try. First of all, they are Branson royalty, responsible for the original boom that put Branson on the map. Secondly, these are truly talented families that seem to have an endless repertoire of songs, instruments, and jokes. And finally, they're just nice people. When the lights go down and you see them at the local grocery store or Home Depot, you'll learn what Branson natives are all about: family, fun, and friendliness.

Presleys' Country Jubilee
2920 W. 76 Country Blvd., Branson
417-334-4874
presleys.com

Branson's Famous Baldknobbers
645 MO-165, Branson
417-231-4999
baldknobbers.com

SING, DANCE, AND DINE
ON THE *SHOWBOAT BRANSON BELLE*

If Dixieland decor, mouthwatering meals, and stunning musical numbers sound like a fantastic night out, then *Showboat Branson Belle* is just the ticket. I prefer the sunset cruise, but I admit it's difficult to drag myself away from the dining room delights to walk the promenade deck and take in the scenery. I don't want to unduly influence you, but as of 2017 the *Belle* had the best show in Branson, as far as I'm concerned. The talent surpassed my expectations, and the sampler of music through the decades was a treat for young and old. We nearly licked the plates clean, the food was so good, and we were dancing in the aisles and off the gangplank all the way home!

4800 MO-165, Branson
800-775-2628
silverdollarcity.com/showboat-branson

TIP

Spring for table seating on the main floor; it has the best view for the show. Should you get seated in the tiered areas behind a pillar, just ask to be moved. The staff is very accommodating, and they will make sure you get a good seat!

PADDLE LAKE TANEYCOMO
ON A MAIN STREET LAKE CRUISE

There's something magical about an old paddlewheel boat. The *Lake Queen* cruises up and down Lake Taneycomo (which still feels like the original White River), while the captain points out original Branson landmarks and the odd hidden waterfall along the banks. Passengers have also spied American bald eagles, blue herons, foxes, coyote, and mink. It is only from here that you can see the Branson Landing's majestic fountain and fire show from the waterside, and it is an unforgettable experience.

If you long for something a little more private, consider chartering the company's exclusive one-hundred-foot yacht, the *Landing Princess*, for your group or event.

9 Branson Landing Blvd., Branson
417-239-3980
mainstreetlakecruises.com

PLAY THE NEWEST GAME IN TOWN
AT ARCADE CITY

Even more lights and music are coming from the Branson Landing with the new Arcade City. Your thumbs will be twitching for a chance to tap into these fun games—whether you want to reclaim your status as the Galaga master or try your hand at one of the new games. The arcade is fair on its prices and generous with its prizes, making it a perfect stop for the whole family. Plus, being on the Branson Landing puts you close to eating and shopping, so you can make a day of it.

Check the website for specials, such as the Smash Faceoff between Mr. and Ms. Pac-Man for Valentine's Day and more!

715 Branson Landing Blvd., Branson
417-203-4150
facebook.com/ArcadeCityBranson

OUTDOOR AND RECREATION

WHEEL IT OR GO ON THE FLY
AT DOGWOOD CANYON

Dogwood Canyon Nature Park is an amazing place to explore the beauty of the Ozarks in its ideal state. The park is carefully landscaped to showcase native plants and allow access to the river, and visitors can cycle along the paved paths (bring your own bike or rent one there) or walk. Head down to the bank to try your hand at catch-and-release fly-fishing . . . and get a guide if you need one. It's not only peaceful and picturesque but also, with links to outdoor titan Bass Pro, a luxury experience.

There are fees to enjoy the park, so call ahead to check about bike rentals and access. We were able to see most sights on level ground (with two small children) in an afternoon's ride. More intrepid adventurers can cycle the entire route clear into Arkansas.

2038 W. State Hwy. 86, Lampe
800-225-6343
dogwoodcanyon.org

FLOAT YOUR CARES AWAY
IN A KAYAK

Our three lakes are perfect for water adventures, and one of the most accessible is kayaking. Visitors have long enjoyed canoeing along the Kings River and James River and on all three area lakes. With slimmer, more manageable kayaks, your opportunities are even greater for getting an upclose look at Ozark beauty. You can drift along the rocky bluffs and look for waterfalls. Watch local residents, such as blue heron, stalk their prey under overhanging trees. See parts of Branson from behind the scenes, such as the docks and old equipment just south of the Branson Landing. Or find a quiet cove and reconnect with the whole family.

5403 State Hwy. 165, Branson
417-336-2811
kayakbranson.com

GO UNDERGROUND
AT MARVEL CAVE

The biggest spelunking experience in the area is certainly Marvel Cave, located at Silver Dollar City. Five hundred feet below ground is a winding labyrinth of tunnels and rooms that have yet to be fully explored. The hour-long tour takes you down hundreds of steps from the entrance to the Cathedral Room—once the site of concerts, dances, weddings, and the odd hot-air balloon flight—and continues with a fascinating look at the area's geological wonders and unique cave-related history.

A newer addition to the daily tours is the evening lantern tour, which really makes you feel like a nineteenth-century explorer! The regular tour is free with the price of park admission, but the lantern-lit tour requires reservations and a small fee.

Not planning on a theme park this trip? You can still experience an Ozark cave at several area caverns, the closest being Talking Rocks Cavern just past Silver Dollar City and Lost Canyon Cave at Top of the Rock just south of Branson.

Marvel Cave
Silver Dollar City
399 Silver Dollar City Pkwy., Branson
800-475-9370
silverdollarcity.com

Talking Rocks Cavern
423 Fairy Cave Ln., Branson West
417-272-3366
talkingrockscavern.com

Lost Canyon Cave
Top of the Rock
190 Top of the Rock Rd., Ridgedale
417-335-2777
topoftherock.com

GET A HOLE IN ONE
PLAYING PUTT-PUTT

For many, playing miniature golf is a vacation tradition. Who can resist the rolling greens, the oversized decorations, the kooky themes, and the chance to crow about your victory over friends and family? More than a dozen putt-putt courses dot the Branson area, and each has its own unique draw. Go back to the fifties, visit a pirate's cove or the dinosaur era, or take it indoors at Grand Country Resort's glow-in-the-dark course. It's your play!

Back to the 50's Mini Golf
2801 E. State Hwy. 76, Branson
417-334-7001

Pirate's Cove Adventure Golf
2901 Green Mountain Dr., Branson
417-336-6606
piratescove.net/branson

Professor Hacker's Lost Treasure Golf
3346 W. 76 Country Blvd., Branson
417-332-0889
losttreasuregolf.com/miniature-golf-courses/
branson-mini-golf-courses/lost-treasure-golf-branson

Professor Hacker's Dinosaur Canyon
2501 Green Mountain Dr., Branson
417-332-0887
losttreasuregolf.com/miniature-golf-courses/
branson-mini-golf-courses/dinosaur-canyon/

Grand Country Resort (multiple courses)
1945 W. 76 Country Blvd., Branson
888-514-1088
grandcountry.com/fun-spot/mini-golf#ms

PADDLEBOAT OR PADDLEBOARD
ON TABLE ROCK LAKE

The still waters around Big Cedar Lodge are ideal for grabbing a paddleboat with a friend or striking out on a paddleboard. Sure, it's a slow way to get around the water, but that's the point. Examine every pebble; contemplate each tree. We like to paddle up from the marina to view Devil's Pool from the bottom, then turn around and get a quick snack back at the dock. Quiet, calm, and powered by you, it's a great way to feel your tensions ripple away in your wake.

(Just remember to untie the boat from the dock *after* you get in. You don't want it slipping out from under you. The lake waters are mighty cold in October . . . just sayin'.)

190 Top of the Rock Rd., Ridgedale
417-335-2777
bigcedar.com/activities/bent-hook-marina-en.html

CRUISE LAKE TANEYCOMO
ON A PONTOON BOAT

I have to admit, this is one of my favorite family activities. Starting at Fall Creek Marina, just below Table Rock Dam, you can cruise all the way to Branson Landing, hop ashore for lunch, and boat back to the marina in just a few hours. Early mornings, the fog sits over the lake and leaves you feeling like the only thing on the water. As the sun peeps out, the fog burns off and reveals many beautiful homes near the bank with private docks. Farther on, a hidden waterfall may appear, or birds enjoying a hunt for waterbugs. Soon you will drift under the expanse of the Taneycomo Bridge. Or, take all day and explore the nooks and crannies of the Ozark hills clear up to Rockaway Beach. Save money and split the cost of the boat rental with family or friends—just make sure your captain is over the age of eighteen!

1 Fall Creek Dr., Branson
800-562-6636
fallcreekmarina.com

TAKE IT TO THE TOP
AT INSPIRATION TOWER

Get your camera ready, because there is no view like the view from the top of Inspiration Tower. Two hundred thirty feet tall, with 4,400 square feet of glass, the tower offers panoramic views from all sides that will take your breath away. Glass elevators will take you up and down . . . or dare to launch yourself from the top via the Vigilante Extreme ZipRider.

5586 W. Hwy. 76, Branson
417-334-4191
theshepherdofthehills.com/inspiration-tower

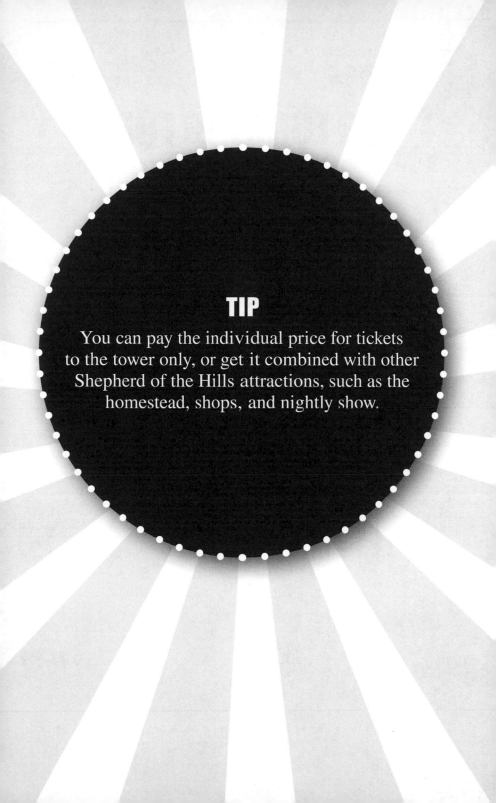

TIP

You can pay the individual price for tickets to the tower only, or get it combined with other Shepherd of the Hills attractions, such as the homestead, shops, and nightly show.

GO LOOKING FOR BIGFOOT

This offroading adventure will have you on the edge of your (truck) seat as you bounce through the Ozark hills. Off the beaten path, you'll love the twists and turns and the fun of looking for the mythological beast. What a wild way to see the backwoods of Branson. Away from the pavement and bright lights you'll discover the original attraction of the Ozarks: its natural beauty. Weave through the oaks, hickory, cedar, and pines and negotiate rock outcroppings and low-water creeks. Don't worry—you're with professionals!

3608 US Hwy. 76, Branson
800-562-2416
bransonbigfoot.com

FIND YOUR ADVENTURE
AT WOLFE MOUNTAIN

If maximum adrenaline is at the top of your list, get over to Wolfe Mountain and experience the amazing zipline and canopy tours, walking trail, and Snowflex park. This is truly the best of the best in the Ozarks for exploring the tops of the trees and the rolling hills. Unlike other attractions, Wolfe Mountain, just north of Branson on Highway 65, is open year-round . . . including the snow-tubing area, which is a real blast in any weather. At this adventure park, you will see how wilderness meets innovation with its state-of-the-art design. Combo tickets are definitely the way to go so you don't miss a thing. Look out below!

2339 US Hwy. 65, Walnut Shade
417-561-0699
wolfemountainbranson.com

RIDE THE WHEEL
ON THE BRANSON FERRIS WHEEL

A relatively new addition to southwest Missouri, the Branson Ferris Wheel enjoyed a former life at the end of Chicago's Navy Pier. At 150 feet tall, the Ferris wheel allows up to six riders in each of forty gondolas to get a panoramic bird's-eye view of Branson and beyond. And while most Ferris wheels are best enjoyed in daylight, this one is really a treat after dark. More than 16,000 LED lights have been added to the structure to put on "Electrify: A Music and Light Spectacular." Shows are nightly on the hour, weather permitting, and can be seen from some distance away.

3345 W. 76 Country Blvd., Branson
417-334-1612
bransontracks.com

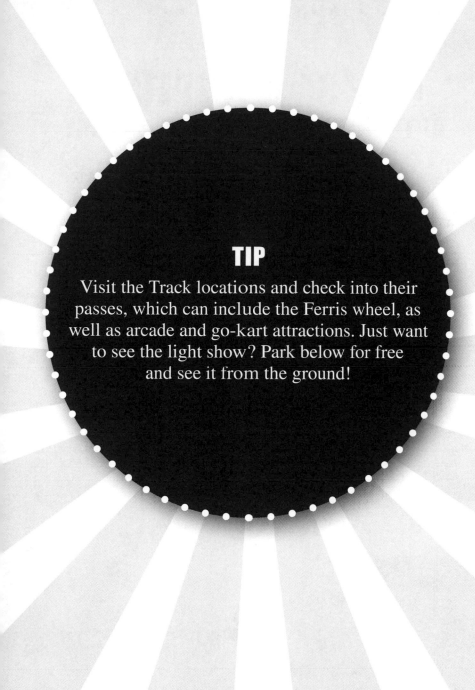

TIP

Visit the Track locations and check into their passes, which can include the Ferris wheel, as well as arcade and go-kart attractions. Just want to see the light show? Park below for free and see it from the ground!

HELP SAVE A SPECIES
AT THE NATIONAL TIGER SANCTUARY

Awe-inspiring is just one word to describe the experience of being in the presence of the world's biggest cats. Tigers, lions, leopards, mountain lions/panthers, and more are cared for in spacious habitats that focus on animal comfort, care, and rehabilitation after rescue. NTS has a unique range of tours available that include feeding the animals, behind-the-scenes secrets, and even a Tigers by Twilight after-dark option that will leave you breathless. Educational, fun, and thrilling is all in a day's work with the tigers.

518 State Hwy. BB, Saddlebrooke
417-587-3633
nationaltigersanctuary.org

SLEEP IN A TREE
AT BRANSON TREEHOUSE ADVENTURES

Imagine nestling in luxury perched among the branches of a mighty oak or hickory tree. You can do just that at Branson Treehouse Adventures, just south of Branson in a beautiful park-like setting. There are several styles to choose from, each with a unique look, but all with the peace and tranquility of the forest.

When you're ready to come back to earth, check out the park amenities, such as basketball, volleyball, croquet, and a horseshoe pit, pool, playground, and campfire. I can't think of a better way to reconnect with family, nature, and yourself.

159 Acorn Acres Ln., Branson West
417-338-2500
bransontreehouseadventures.com

BEAT THE HEAT (OR COLD)
AT FRITZ'S ADVENTURE

Too hot, cold, or rainy? Don't settle for a boring day—go on an adventure at Fritz's Adventure, an indoor fun park. If you can do it "out there," you can do it in here: rock-wall climbing, underground tunnel exploration, ropes, bridges, ziplines, trampolines, mazes, a laser agility course, treehouses, slides, and more are all housed in this giant complex on the Strip. The only real question is, which one of you will wear out first?

1425 W. Hwy. 76, Branson
417-320-6138
fritzsadventure.com

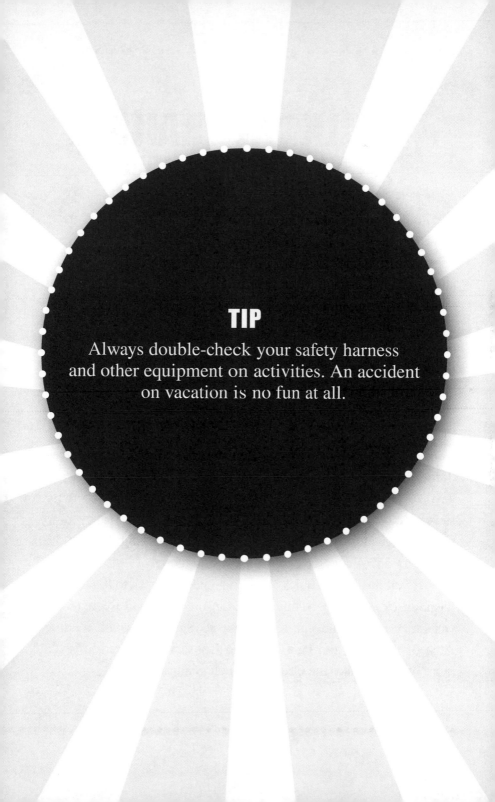

TIP

Always double-check your safety harness and other equipment on activities. An accident on vacation is no fun at all.

WALK THE TRAILS
OF AN OZARK MOUNTAIN

The oldest outdoor adventure there is—walking the trails made by those who came before. The Ozark Mountains are crisscrossed with paths made by Native Americans and settlers, and you can traverse some of these in our fabulous parks and reserves. Crunch through fallen leaves under a canopy of trees, climb over rock ledges, explore a Civil War cave, stumble upon an old homestead, and rest beneath a waterfall. All of these are possible just minutes from the bustle of Branson.

My go-to back-to-nature break is Lakeside Forest Wilderness Area, right in the heart of Branson. From the parking area, take the main trail back to the old homestead. From there, you can take several branching paths. One will lead down stone steps placed decades ago to a small cove and waterfall, with a hidden cave just beyond. (Just remember that you *will* need to walk back up those steps!) Another path leads to sweeping views of Lake Taneycomo and all the way to Arkansas. A third has you ducking through the woods for a firsthand look at area flora and fauna.

If you just want a quick stroll that gets you back to the car in a flash, check out the park trails on Branson Parks and Recreation's website. For longer adventures, try Busiek State Forest and Wildlife Area or the Ruth and Paul Henning Conservation Area for even more of what makes the Ozarks a timeless attraction.

Lakeside Forest Wilderness Area
412 Owen Ln., Branson
417-335-2368
bransonparksandrecreation.com

Busiek State Forest and Wildlife Area
Highway 65, Highlandville, 16.5
miles north of Branson
417-895-6880
nature.mdc.mo.gov/discover-nature/
places/busiek-sf-and-wa

Ruth and Paul Henning Conservation Area
3601 Shepherd of the Hills Expy., Branson
417-895-6880
nature.mdc.mo.gov/discover-nature/
places/henning-ruth-and-paul-ca

FALL FOR FUN
AT MCKENNA'S PUMPKIN PATCH

The McKenna Family Farm is tucked just off Highway 65, but you feel like you've traveled to the country, and to a simpler time. Not only are there seasonal crops for sale and a charming log church open for weddings, but the fall season really shows off the farm. This is an annual favorite for my family, but the details change each year. At first, the jumping pillow and corn maze were the highlights. Next time it was the pony swings and big haystack. But we can't miss the hayride, baby farm animals, big slides, or giant gerbil wheels. McKenna's is the wholesome family fun place you've been looking for.

Many offerings are seasonal, so be sure to call ahead for what is current and for open days and times.

3265 State Hwy. F, Branson
417-593-3159
mckennafamilyfarm.com

GET A DAM VIEW
AT DEWEY SHORT VISITOR CENTER

A new addition to the shores of Table Rock Lake, the Dewey Short Visitor Center is packed with fun and educational activities. At the center, which is entirely free, visitors can learn about the construction of Table Rock Dam, take in the spectacular views from the observation deck, explore the aquariums and exhibits, and walk the trails surrounding the complex. This is a hidden gem that should not be missed if you want to see how an engineering feat changed the landscape and the future of an entire region.

4500 State Hwy. 165, Branson
501-340-1943
swl.usace.army.mil/Missions/Recreation/Lakes/
Table-Rock-Lake/Recreation-Activities

LEAN INTO IT
AT BRANSON SEGWAY AND ADVENTURE CENTER

Tired of driving? It's time to try something different. A Segway is not just the vehicle of choice for mall cops—it's also a fun way to get outside. The Adventure Center has a free-range track so you can experiment with the steering mechanism (hint: it's your own balance). And who knows? You might find the skills for a new career at your local mall.

You can find the Segway and Adventure Center just off the Strip near St. James Winery and the Baldknobber Theater. Call ahead for operation times, as weather may affect your ability to participate.

299 State Hwy. 165, Branson
417-336-2744
bransonsegway.com

GO BACK IN TIME
AT SILVER DOLLAR CITY

Lots of individual must-dos scattered throughout this book can only be found at Silver Dollar City. It's the most bang for your buck and has attractions you will not find at any other theme park—part 1800s village, part roller coaster thrill, with a generous helping of great food and music. You haven't really experienced Branson until you go to Silver Dollar City.

To get the real olden-days experience, head for the craftspeople who portray living history in costume, practicing the old ways of blacksmithing, glass blowing, candle making, baking, pottery, basketry, leather work, and a host of other crafts. The Silver Dollar Saloon should be at the top of your list for shows. Keep a keen eye out for exhibits and plaques throughout the park explaining points of interest from yesteryear.

Just do it, y'all.

399 Silver Dollar City Pkwy., Branson
800-475-9370
silverdollarcity.com

VISIT MOONSHINE BEACH

Ditch the pool and head for the lake! Once a local secret, Moonshine Beach on the freshwater shores of Table Rock Lake is now easy to find and well maintained by the park system. Parking is five dollars, and you can stay all day (although I recommend bringing a picnic and settling in for the sunset . . . it's spectacular!).

Keep in mind that freshwater temperatures can fluctuate. Summer is the best time for a visit, but take care to protect yourself from the sun. Rays reflected off the beautiful waters of Table Rock Lake can make for a nasty sunburn. In fall and spring, water temperatures can be in the upper fifties, so it may be a good time to have that waterside picnic and practice skipping rocks.

3778 State Hwy. 165, Branson
501-340-1950
recreation.gov/camping/moonshine-beach-rec-area/r/
campgroundDetails.do?contractCode=NRSO&parkId=75236

MAKE A SPLASH
AT A WATER PARK

Summertime means swimming, sunbathing, and water-tubing, and Branson is bursting with places to do all three. White Water is the largest and oldest water theme park, with ties to Silver Dollar City (read here, "combo ticket"). Castle Rock has an indoor water park for hotel guests that is also open to the public. Splash Country has both indoor and outdoor features and offers the best bang for a family buck. Whether you want endless thrills or a lazy river loop, these water parks have something for everyone.

White Water
3505 W. State Hwy. 76, Branson
800-532-7529
silverdollarcity.com

Splash Country
1945 W. 76 Country Blvd., Branson
888-505-4096
grandcountry.com

Castle Rock
3001 Green Mountain Dr., Branson
888-273-3919
castlerockbranson.com

HIT THE LINKS
ON THE GOLF COURSE

Golfers love the challenge of our rolling hills and trickling streams. It's hard to say which course is the most beautiful, or which the most difficult. Serious players will want to try them all!

Don Gardner Golf Course is a free, nine-hole, par three course operated by the city.

201 Compton Dr., Branson
417-337-8510
bransonparksandrecreation.com/page.php?id=15

Branson Hills Golf Club
100 N. Payne Stewart Dr., Branson
417-337-2963
bransonhillsgolfclub.com

The Pointe at Pointe Royale
142 Clubhouse Dr., Branson
417-334-4477
pointeroyale.com

Thousand Hills Golf Resort
245 S. Wildwood Dr., Branson
417-336-5873
thousandhills.com

Holiday Hills Golf Club
630 E. Rockford Dr., Branson
417-334-4838
holidayhills.com

Buffalo Ridge Springs
1001 Branson Creek Blvd., Hollister
417-339-5430
bigcedar.com/golf/buffalo-ridge-en.html

Top of the Rock Golf Course
190 Top of the Rock Rd., Ridgedale
417-339-5344
topoftherock.com/top-of-the-rock-golf-course

LedgeStone Country Club at StoneBridge Village
1600 LedgeStone Way, Branson West
417-335-8187
ledgestonegolf.com

BE AN OUTDOOR PRO
AT BASS PRO SHOPS

The world's largest sporting goods stores are more than a mecca for fishing, camping, and golfing equipment. They are an architectural pleasure, fitting into the natural landscape, with large timber construction and rock and water features. The Branson Landing location has an impressive wall aquarium and display of fishing boats and ATVs—and it is open 364 days a year! The White River Outpost is the southern-most anchor store for the Landing, with ample parking on that side and a free trolley to other areas of downtown.

1 Bass Pro Dr., Branson
417-243-5200
stores.basspro.com/us/mo/branson/1-bass-pro-dr.html

TIP

For more Bass Pro entertainment, visit the headquarters store in Springfield, a thirty-minute drive north.

RELEASE A NEW BUTTERFLY

Perched on the end of Highway 76 is a large domed building you might mistake for another theater, but it houses something unique, a show more breathtaking than any choreographed program. The Butterfly Palace is home to thousands of tropical butterflies from all over the world. Stroll through the habitat and let them land on your shoulders. Take a close-up photo as you watch them feed. Relax to the live dulcimer playing of musician John Corbin Goldsberry. And the best part is the opportunity to release the newly emerged butterflies as they spread their wings.

The habitat experience includes a 3-D film and many other animals on display, as well as an intriguing mirror maze, science center, and fun obstacle course. It's a great value, with all-day admission and a three-day wristband that lets you come back for more.

4106 W. Hwy. 76, Branson
417-332-2231
thebutterflypalace.com

FEED THE FISH
AT SHEPHERD OF THE HILLS
FISH HATCHERY

A wonderful (free!) stop just below Table Rock Dam is the largest Missouri Department of Conservation fish hatchery. View the various tanks of trout that will soon enter the waters of Lake Taneycomo. Visitors can feed some of the 400,000 pounds of rainbow and brown trout produced each year, view the exhibits inside the conservation center, and walk the many trails threading the banks of the lake. There's a boat ramp if you'd like to fish anytime year-round and pavilions and picnic tables for gatherings large and small.

633 Hatchery Rd., Branson
417-348-1305
nature.mdc.mo.gov/discover-nature/places/
shepherd-hills-fish-hatchery

PASS OUT PEANUT BUTTER TO PARAKEETS

I'm a big fan of zoos and animal rescue efforts in general, but the Promised Land Zoo is unique. Rated a Top Twenty-Five Zoo in the United States by TripAdvisor, this park is very hands-on and full of heart. Start with the parakeet encounter and thrill to the hundreds of budgies ready to perch on the treat stick and gather at your feet. Guests can pet many of the animals, and bottle feedings are a daily privilege. The live animal shows are informative, and there are options for one-on-one encounters with select species. Just when your feet are starting to feel the effects of your adventures, it's time to experience all new animals with the Drive Thru Safari. Every visit to the Promised Land Zoo promises a good time.

2751 Shepherd of the Hills Expy., Branson
417-337-9453
plzoo.com

GET IN A FESTIVE(AL) MOOD

It seems like Branson is always having a festival of some kind. From fireworks to fiddling and Elvis to Easter eggs, each season brings a special excitement to town. If you are heading to Silver Dollar City, you will find specific festival foods and entertainment in the park, but for other festival locations and details, visit explorebranson.com.

SPRING
Branson Elvis Festival
Great Hollister Easter Egg Hunt
Festival of Wonder (SDC)
Branson Music Fest
Bluegrass and BBQ (SDC)

SUMMER
Plumb Nellie Days
Star-Spangled Summer (SDC)
Fireburst (Fourth of July)
Branson Fiddle Festival
Southern Gospel Picnic (SDC)

FALL
Autumn Daze Arts, Crafts, and Music Festival
Hollister Grape and Fall Festival
National Crafts and Cowboy Festival (SDC)
Veterans Day Parade

WINTER
Most Wonderful Time of the Year Parade
An Old Time Christmas (SDC)
Adoration Christmas Parade

GO UP, UP, AND AWAY
IN A STEAMPUNK BALLOON

Like a balloon ride at the county fair or something out of *The Wizard of Oz*, getting a bird's-eye view of Branson was never so exciting. To passersby at night it looks like a full golden moon, but to those lucky enough to step inside the basket at Parakeet Pete's Steampunk Balloon, it is the means to get airborne. Take in the 360-degree view from 188 feet in the air, with a unique perspective on Lake Taneycomo and the Branson Landing.

You can access the balloon at the northern end of the Branson Landing, outside Belk and Black Oak Grill. There is plenty of parking on this side of the Landing, with a free trolley to other parts of the downtown area.

1113 Branson Landing Blvd., Branson
800-712-7654
bransonlandingattractions.com

TIP

Another quirky way to see the Landing from above is to try Parakeet Pete's other attraction, the Waterfront Zipline. No harness required—you'll be pulled to the top in a secure seat and then let go to fly over the lake back to the boardwalk.

TAKE A RIDE ON SPARKY
THE DOWNTOWN TROLLEY

There's something magical about riding on a trolley or streetcar. Most cities charge a fee to ride, but in Branson you can ride "Sparky" for free to any of the thirteen stops throughout historic downtown Branson and the Landing. You might hear a few theories about how Sparky got its name, but the truth is that a third grader won a naming contest, honoring Pearl "Sparky" Spurlock, who ran a tour and taxi business in the 1920s.

The trolley runs seven days a week (except in January and February, when it runs only Thursday through Sunday). It's a fun and informative way to see the old town. You can do it in about forty-five minutes if you ride the full circuit, or just go from Main Street to the Landing in about five minutes. There's a video playing on board that will tell you some of the history, or you can just take in the sights and enjoy the ride.

112 W. College St., Branson
417-334-1548
ridesparky.com

SOAR OVER BRANSON
IN A HELICOPTER

It's the ultimate city tour. Buzzing high over the Ozark Mountains, you'll see the serpentine paths of Lake Taneycomo, magnificent Table Rock Dam, and all of Branson laid out like a miniature village. Companies offer multiple price ranges and cover different areas, so call around for the tour that fits your style. Still on my to-do list are the dinner tours and the I Pilot option of Chopper Charter. Besides the thrill of being in a helicopter, they'll let you fly yourself and eat a meal in the clouds.

Branson Helicopter Tours
3309 MO-76, Branson
417-593-0149
branson-helicoptertours.com

Chopper Charter
469 Blue Sky Ln., Hollister
(Tours start across from Presleys' Theatre on the Strip.)
417-332-1545
choppercharter.com

TAKE A SWING
AT THE BATTING CAGES

Practice your major league skills at the Track's four batting cages. Set up to throw four different speeds for baseball and softball—you can get twenty pitches at a time or rent the cage by the half hour so everybody gets a try. Put me in, coach!

Be sure to ask about the combo tickets to get the best price if you plan to ride go-karts or visit one of the arcades. The Track has multiple locations, so pick your favorite activities from the "menu" to get the most bang for your buck.

3525 W. 76 Country Blvd., Branson
417-334-1612
bransontracks.com/rides/battingcages

CRUISE IN THE CAR OF YOUR DREAMS
AT THE BRANSON AUCTION

It only happens twice a year—the chance to own the ride of a lifetime. Each April and October car connoisseurs descend on the Branson Convention Center to peruse the finest in automotive engineering at the Branson Auction. For more than forty years, Jim and Kathy Cox have been sharing their rare, vintage domestic and foreign models from all over the world. Call for exact show dates, but in the meantime visit them online. Their website offers live streaming of the event; to catch a taste of previous sales, check out their video section to learn about the 1926 Model T, '55 Bel Air, and Jaguar XKE and see which one Enzo Ferrari hailed as "the most beautiful car ever built."

There's an entry fee—with a military discount—for one- or two-day passes, but it's worth the price of admission just to get a glimpse of these beauties. There's plenty to explore at both the show and the Branson Landing just steps away.

800-335-3063
bransonauction.com

Overnight reservations:
Hilton Branson Convention Center
200 E. Main St., Branson
417-336-5400

MAKE A DAY OF IT
WITH AREA DAY TRIPS

Branson has an endless supply of thrills and diversions, but sometimes you want to get out of town and go for a drive. North, south, east, or west, there are scenic views and quaint towns, shopping and dining adventures, and a new memory around every corner. Take a day trip and see what the Ozarks are all about!

Springfield
Battlefield Mall
Springfield Art Museum
Wonders of Wildlife National Museum and Aquarium
Bass Pro Shops
Springfield Botanical Gardens at Nathanael Greene/
Close Memorial Park and Mizumoto
Japanese Stroll Garden
Wilson's Creek National Battlefield

Forsyth and Rockaway Beach
Scenic overlooks
Thrift stores and flea markets
Yummy Donuts
Kim's BBQ Shack

Mansfield
Laura Ingalls Wilder Historic Home and Museum

Diamond
George Washington Carver National Monument

Carthage
Precious Moments Chapel

Eureka Springs, Arkansas
Historic downtown
The Great Passion Play

CULTURE AND HISTORY

SAMPLE
OLD-FASHIONED TREATS
AT COLLEGE OF THE OZARKS

I really can't stress enough how much you need to visit the College of the Ozarks. I know . . . touring a college sounds boring, but I promise this one is different. At one of the country's only "working" colleges, students graduate debt-free by working on campus to offset tuition costs. This means that the college is self-sufficient, training young people in the greenhouse, dairy barn, mill, weaving studio, on-site restaurant and hotel, and, of course, the Fruitcake and Jelly Kitchen. Homemade jellies, fruitcakes, and candies are created on site and sold in the gift shop. You can tour most of the facilities (*free!*), try a sample, and get all your questions answered.

Much more than a standard living history museum, this community is living the present by adapting old ways to new methods of commerce and education. Plan to spend a couple of hours wandering the beautiful grounds—stroll around Tranquility Lake and step inside the peaceful chapel and the one-room schoolhouse on your way to Point Lookout.

100 Opportunity Ave., Point Lookout
800-222-0525, cofo.edu

TIP

For under ten dollars you can enjoy another couple of hours at the Ralph Foster Museum, where high-quality exhibits include early settlement, the region's animals, stunning antiques, and the *Beverly Hillbillies* truck. Call ahead for operating times, and ask about the senior and homeschooler discounts.

SEE THE STORY THAT STARTED IT ALL
AT SHEPHERD OF THE HILLS

The cultural and historical importance of the Shepherd of the Hills Homestead Adventure Park cannot be overstated. If it weren't for Ol' Matt and Aunt Molly, the Ozarks would still be hidden from the world. Walking through their cabin, seeing the loom where Aunt Molly wove her many rugs, poking around the blacksmith forge . . . it brings the past to life in a way many of us have lost in our family histories.

What makes this little history stop so exciting is the addition of working craftspeople, a trip up Inspiration Tower (and ziplining down again, if you choose), the sing-along Chuckwagon Dinner, and the nighttime amphitheater show depicting Harold Bell Wright's original story, which follows the loves and losses of the people who once roamed these hills. You can stay for an hour or two, but the best plan is to get there about 2 p.m.; explore the grounds, homestead, and tower; and then have dinner and head to the night show.

5586 W. Hwy. 76, Branson
417-334-4191
theshepherdofthehills.com

BE PART OF A LOST ART
AT BRANSON MILL CRAFT VILLAGE

It's a sad fact that the skills our ancestors used on a daily basis are a dying art. Few people can weave a basket, dip their own candles, or design a rocking chair from willow branches. The Branson Mill Craft Village is a comfortable indoor center for working craftspeople to show and sell their wares.

Admittedly, it is a sanitized version of the past, but it's an excellent place to view contemporary artisans and pick up some local pieces of art. More a craft "mall" than a mill, Branson Mill will entertain shoppers who enjoy browsing, while those who want to delve more deeply into the process can watch the masters at work.

3300 N. Gretna Rd., Branson
417-334-8436
bransonmill.com

TRAVEL TO THE 1800s
AT SILVER DOLLAR CITY

"The City," or SDC, as the locals call it, should be at the top of your list. Yes, it's pricey. Yes, it's a theme park. But Silver Dollar City is unique among other amusement venues. The reproduction village and costumed workers contribute to the educational vibe of the park. Dozens of shops, shows, dining options, roving entertainers, and rides for all ages make this more than a day trip. This is the jackpot for watching craftspeople at work—blacksmiths, candymakers, glassblowers, potters, woodcarvers, weavers—and that doesn't include the various festivals throughout the year. No other place will give you such an immersive experience of Ozark history, crafts, and music. Forget about the money and make some great memories.

399 Silver Dollar City Pkwy., Branson
800-475-9370
silverdollarcity.com

TIPS

Don't bother paying for premium parking or fancy food or ride packages. They are a waste of money and don't give you any significant advantages over the regular offerings. (The only exception here is getting a front-of-the-line pass for rides on busy holiday weekends or summer dates. If you're just here for the thrill rides, this might be worth it for you.)

Definitely take the Marvel Cave tour, as it is exceptional among cave tours and bursting with history. (Just make sure you are fit enough for an hour's walk and can tolerate some confined spaces.)

Check on the After 3:00, Next Day Free price break. You basically get a day and a half for the price of one. (And if you stay for the free night show, you're getting even more!)

If you are planning to visit SDC's partners— White Water, *Showboat Branson Belle*, or the Wilderness Cabins and Campground—call about their combo tickets.

GO WHERE THE BUFFALO ROAM
AT DOGWOOD CANYON

For me, Dogwood Canyon is a dream day trip. On a perfect spring or autumn day, there is nothing better than cycling through the bottom of the canyon along the water's edge. Unless it is perfecting your fly-fishing skills. Or it could be the trail rides on horseback or ATV. But for the ultimate adventure, take the tram ride through the entire park, crossing the state line into Arkansas and viewing bison and elk up close and personal. It's a gorgeous wedding and photo spot, but more importantly it is a place to remind us of what nature can be when it's in a cultivated and honored state.

There are fees to access the park, so call ahead for details on your preferred activity. Reservations are preferred for the tram tours. And take your camera! This place is beautiful any time of year, but fall is spectacular.

2038 W. State Hwy. 86, Lampe
800-225-6343
dogwoodcanyon.org

GRIND IT
AT EDWARDS MILL

A wonderful piece of Ozark history can be found on the grounds of College of the Ozarks at Edwards Mill. Powered by a twelve-foot water wheel, the mill, operated by student workers, grinds whole -grain meal and flour just as it was done more than a hundred years ago. I feel a special kinship to the collection of mill wheels on display around the building, as one of them is from my little town's original mill. The machinery is impressive to see in action, the mill itself is a piece of the past, and upstairs is a weaving studio where students craft rugs, shawls, and placemats—all for sale in the college gift shop, along with the meal and flour from the mill. Don't miss the opportunity to walk behind the structure, where a beautiful millpond with resident ducks hides in perfect tranquility.

Best of all, it's *free*!

Edwards Mill
College of the Ozarks
100 Opportunity Ave., Point Lookout
800-222-0525
cofo.edu

History of the mill
stateoftheozarks.com/Cultural/Craftsmanship/
MillsOzarks/EdwardsMill.html

● ●

TAKE YE OLDE STROLL
IN HISTORIC DOWNTOWN HOLLISTER

While Branson has boomed its way into the twenty-first century, historic downtown Hollister is quietly grooving to yesteryear. Once it was the end of the railway line, depositing Chicago's elite at lodges and inns that perched on the hillside, and it played host to Babe Ruth and his team for spring training. It was a bustling crossroads for business when Branson was in its infancy. Now you can stroll along Downing Street, taking in the old architecture, antique shops, beautifully restored inn and pub, and train depot. It's a calmer, more sedate experience that is best ended by a stop at Vintage Paris to have a glass of wine and listen to some local musicians on the patio.

312 Esplanade St., Hollister
417-334-3262
cityofhollister.com

BE A KID AGAIN
AT THE WORLD'S LARGEST TOY MUSEUM

We all have that favorite iconic toy from our childhoods, and chances are you can relive the memories at the World's Largest Toy Museum. The sheer number of objects housed within is staggering. There is a guaranteed smile waiting within as you discover the fun from your past.

More than a million toys are crammed onto the shelves and floors of this impressive museum. Focusing mostly on the 1940s through the 1970s, the museum lets you reminisce about childhood hours spent with train sets, Roy Rogers cap guns, cast-iron cars, and vintage lunch boxes. It's definitely a look-but-don't-touch kind of place, so this is an activity best suited for older children and the young at heart.

3609 W. Hwy. 76, Branson
417-332-1499
worldslargesttoymuseum.com

SEE HOW A RIVER BECAME A LAKE
AT TABLE ROCK DAM

Completed in 1959, Table Rock Dam forever changed the face of the Ozarks. Its 6,423 feet stretched across the White River and created Table Rock Lake and Lake Taneycomo. Take a fascinating drive across the top of the dam, noting the vastly different views above and below, then pull into the viewing lot on the south side for a closer look. You might catch some more views from Chateau on the Lake and Moonshine Beach on the north side. Or try some of the hiking trails through the state park and catch a glimpse of this magnificent structure through the trees. For more in-depth information and photos of the construction, visit the Dewey Short Visitor Center at the south end of the dam.

Dewey Short Visitor Center
4500 State Hwy. T, Branson
501-340-1943
swl.usace.army.mil/Missions/Recreation/Lakes/
Table-Rock-Lake/Recreation-Activities

GET KRAZY FOR KEWPIES
AT BONNIEBROOK

Ah, Bonniebrook. Truly a hidden gem in the Ozarks, this art gallery, home, and museum is on the National Register of Historic Places and honors the life and work of Rose O'Neill—creator of the Kewpie doll. The home is lovingly preserved from the Art Deco days of O'Neill's time and showcases her work as an illustrator, author, artist, and sculptor. Much more than a memorial to the artist and her world-famous chubby cherub, the house and grounds alone are worth the visit for their beautiful location nestled by a woodland stream.

485 Rose O'Neill Rd., Walnut Shade
417-561-1509
roseoneill.org

RIDE THE RAILS
WITH BRANSON SCENIC RAILWAY

All aboard! The Ozark Zephyr is about to take you on a splendid scenic tour of the Ozark Mountains, 1930s style! I'm a sucker for a train ride, and while this one is a bit short for me (sixty to ninety minutes), it is a privilege to ride in a vintage railway car and feel the rocking of the rails. The train has two routes, dependent on other rail traffic, so you never know which one you will be assigned until you are already on board. The south route is by far the more scenic, with sweeping views of the hills down through Arkansas. But, either way, it is fun to wander the cars, grab a snack in the old dining car, and peek through the overarching windows of the dome car.

206 E. Main St., Branson
417-334-6110
bransontrain.com

GET REVVED UP!
AT THE BRANSON AUTO
AND FARM MUSEUM

I admit to being partial to this particular stop, as it houses one of the cars my parents owned (a 1931 Ford Model A Cabriolet named "Scarlett"). The newly built 90,000-square-foot building is divided evenly between classic cars and tractors and farm machinery. You'll be drooling over everything from Cadillacs to Corvettes, Model Ts to muscle cars.

It's a wonderful tour through time, but especially good to remember on cold or rainy days. You'll find it easily on the Strip, with some of its cars parked out front on display. Be sure to get a photo with your favorite ride (or three!), as pictures are encouraged.

1335 W. Hwy. 76, Branson
417-335-2600
bransonmuseum.com

GET A GLIMPSE OF DAYS GONE BY
AT TITANIC BRANSON

At once poignant and breathtaking, Titanic Branson offers a unique opportunity to touch history—or at least a very good likeness of it. The cabins, hallways, grand staircase, and promenade deck have been recreated to give "passengers" the feeling of being in 1912. View artifacts from the original ship and learn the stories of those who traveled on the ill-fated journey.

Upon entry, you'll be given the name of a real person who sailed on the *Titanic*. As you meander through the exhibits, look for clues to where your passenger bunked, what their life was like aboard the luxury liner, and what fate awaited them. If you're brave, plunge your hand into the icy waters of the interactive area and feel the breeze on the bow of the ship, recreating the Arctic temperatures of that unforgettable night. By the time you depart, you'll have a real understanding of this time capsule in world history, and a brush with the past.

3235 76 Country Blvd., Branson
417-334-9500
titanicbranson.com

BELIEVE IT OR NOT!
AT RIPLEY'S

You may have encountered the wonderful vintage magazines or reruns of the television show that collected oddities from around the world. Now see them housed under one—very unusual—roof. You know you're in for a treat when you pull up to a building that is literally coming apart at the seams. The fantastic architectural design of the museum is a photo-op in itself. But wait till you get inside.

Home of the weird and wonderful, Ripley's will have you scratching your head and marveling at the sheer oddity of the human race. Kids want a chance to see a real shrunken head and make faces in the goofy mirrors. (Who am I kidding? Everyone wants a chance to see a shrunken head and make goofy faces in the mirrors!) Adults appreciate the jade carvings and matchstick art. And everyone gets in on the "world record" fun to locate the smallest, biggest, oldest, tallest, shortest, and one-of-a-kind finds. It's a great way to change the pace of Branson sightseeing or while away a rainy afternoon.

3326 W. State Hwy. 76, Branson
417-337-5300
ripleys.com

COME AND LISTEN TO A STORY 'BOUT A MAN NAMED JED

The Beverly Hillbillies' truck is probably the main attraction for most visitors to the Ralph Foster Museum, but don't miss out on the three floors of exhibits that house an impressive gemstone collection, antique clocks and pocket watches, looms, spinning wheels, Western show costumes, natural history displays, and . . . well, pretty much anything from the 1920s to today.

The one-room Star Schoolhouse is next door, and young and old will enjoy sitting in the old desks and seeing what lessons were in store for long-ago students.

Ask about senior, student, and homeschool discounts!

1 Cultural Ct., Point Lookout
417-690-3407
rfostermuseum.com

TIP

If you have more time, take in the other College of the Ozarks sights, such as the Presbyterian Church, Edwards Mill, Fruitcake and Jelly Kitchen, and Keeter Center.

HAVE A CELEBRITY ENCOUNTER
AT THE HOLLYWOOD WAX MUSEUM

It's the ultimate selfie . . . with Hollywood at your doorstep! Sure, it's kitschy, cheesy, and silly. But it's also good fun. Examine Tom Selleck's mustache up close. Shout "Action!" with Steven Spielberg. Coo with Marilyn Monroe standing over that famous street grate. You'll be walking down memory lane with these fun (and eerily life-like) recreations of celebrities and movie scenes.

It's probably not worth missing one of your priority sights during your vacation, but it's a no-brainer break if you've had enough of the bustle of Branson.

3030 W. 76 Country Blvd., Branson
417-337-8277
hollywoodwaxmuseum.com

SEE THE REAL OZARKS
ON A SCENIC DRIVE

There's no better way to see the beauty of the Ozarks than on a leisurely drive through the country. Branson is perfectly situated at the center of several gorgeous routes (especially in October!), and with gas prices typically lower than in other parts of the United States, it is a pretty economical way to spend an hour or two. Check a website for route specifics and utilize the GPS feature in your car or on your phone to be sure you don't get lost!

My personal favorite? The route through the Mark Twain National Forest east of Branson on Highway 160 between Forsyth and Theodosia. Check out the thrift stores and stop for lunch in Forsyth.

Another great route to try is west of Branson on Highway 86 from Kimberling City to Eagle Rock. This passes Dogwood Canyon and Persimmon Hill Farm.

go-missouri.com/branson/scenic-drives

CRACK YOUR OWN GEODE
AT PREHISTORIC FOSSILS

One visitor explained this unique little place as a "museum that's liquidating its artifacts!" You'll be thrilled at the up-close and personal look at treasures from the past, including gems, minerals, and fossils. And yes, you really can break open your own geode and discover what secrets are held within. The shop is sort of a hidden gem itself, snuggled at the top of the historic downtown district.

Being small means the shop can be quirky and surprising and offer us mere humans a look at rare dinosaurs you won't find in other museums. I especially like the opportunity to touch many of the specimens—something that doesn't happen in stuffier establishments. Don't miss this natural history museum on your next visit to Branson.

101 Veterans Blvd., Branson
417-320-6124
indiana9fossils.com

SHOPPING AND FASHION

SHOP AT THE SOURCE
AT SILVER DOLLAR CITY

There are several shops within Silver Dollar City's theme park where you can watch the finished product form before your eyes. Hazel's Blown and Cut Glass Factory is a top stop, with workers braving the fiery kilns to create these pieces of art. The Blacksmith Shop, Brown's Candy Factory, and Carrie's Candles are other great places to watch traditional crafts come to life—or even try your hand at making them.

It isn't the same as supporting small local businesses, but it is a convenient way to take in varying techniques with friendly artisans who will take the time to explain their craft.

399 Silver Dollar City Pkwy., Branson
800-475-9370
silverdollarcity.com

GET YOUR GLITZ ON
AT THE GRAND VILLAGE SHOPS

Brighter than the night lights of Branson, the sequined, rhinestone-studded, and gilded offerings of Grand Glitz will have you feeling like a star. The Grand Village Shops are a lovely afternoon break in the middle of the Strip, with beautiful fountains and cobblestone pathways that elevate shopping to the indulgent experience it should be. This place invites you to slow down and enjoy the window-shopping experience. I never miss a chance to drop in to T. Charleston's Books and Gifts, and the singing waitstaff at Mel's Hard Luck Diner will make sure you leave with a smile and a song.

2800 W. Hwy. 76, Branson
grandvillageshops.com

BROWSE THE BOARDWALK
AT BRANSON LANDING

Few shopping venues can boast such a relaxing atmosphere. Wedged between historic downtown Branson and Lake Taneycomo is the planned and pristine Branson Landing. Visitors can start at either end of the complex in one of the anchor stores—Bass Pro Shops or Belk—and find dozens of specialty stores and upscale retail shops in between. The promenade that connects the anchors is closed to vehicles, and walking the bricked path with its old-fashioned lamps adds to the atmosphere.

For a breath of fresh air, duck behind the buildings to the winding boardwalk path that follows the banks of the lake. Some of my favorite restaurants are located here, too—Black Oak Grill and Waxy O'Shea's Irish Pub. And be sure to see the fountain show at the center of everything, with shows on the hour.

100 Branson Landing, Branson
417-239-3002
bransonlanding.com

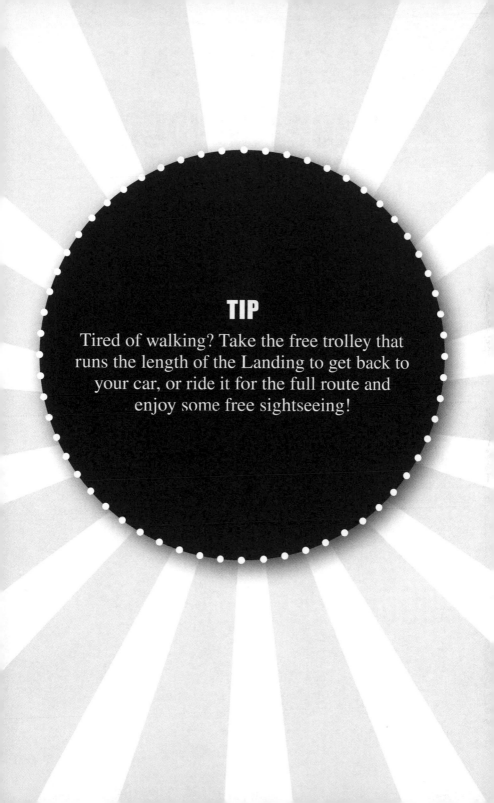

TIP

Tired of walking? Take the free trolley that runs the length of the Landing to get back to your car, or ride it for the full route and enjoy some free sightseeing!

SHOP FOR YOUR RETURN TRIP
WITH A TIMESHARE TOUR

You wouldn't normally consider a ninety-minute sales pitch to be a shopping option, but with so many vacation clubs and timeshare resorts in town, there are some deals to be had. If you aren't worried about your schedule and have a strong resistance to sales pressure, taking a tour can snag you free show and meal tickets, complimentary night stays, and even another whole vacation.

Be wary of long-term payments, maintenance fees, and other fine-print ways to cost you money, but definitely enjoy the beautiful facilities and dare to dream a little. A quick call will get you a tour time at your convenience.

JUST A FEW POSSIBILITIES

Big Cedar Lodge
800-225-6343

Wyndham Resorts
417-336-4993

StoneBridge
417-332-1373

Nantucket
417-338-5006

GET THE
BARGAIN-HUNTING BUG
AT CADWELL'S DOWNTOWN
FLEA MARKET

Cadwell's, in downtown Branson, is a flea market aficionado's dream. Artfully organized and jam-packed with antiques and vintage items of every kind, Cadwell's is a place where you will love getting lost among the aisles. It's ideally situated in historic downtown Branson, which is a great shopping stop of its own. There are lots of restaurants nearby, so relax and take your time to find that one-of-a-kind treasure you've been searching for.

If you love a good flea market, I don't have to say another word because you've already dropped this book and gone.

114 E. Main St., Branson
417-334-5051
facebook.com/pages/Cadwells-Downtown-Flea-Mkt/120759031274404

CUT IT, STAMP IT, AND GLUE IT
AT SCRAPBOOKS FOREVER

I'm going to let you in on a local secret—the best scrapbook and paper arts supply store in Branson! Tucked into a small building on the Strip, this shop is bursting to the seams with ideas and the materials to make them come true. Whether you are into making memory pages or handmade cards, embossing or die-cutting, it has all the tools you'll need. Classes are offered each month, but they fill up fast, so call ahead to reserve your seat. It also carries popular paper brands such as Graphic 45, BoBunny, and Tim Holtz, along with matching stickers and embellishments.

Don't miss the specialty papers and embellishments featuring Missouri and the Ozarks. You won't find them anywhere else!

3010 W. 76 Country Blvd., Branson
417-335-7904
scrapbooksforeverbranson.com

PLAY THAT MOUNTAIN MUSIC
AT CEDAR CREEK DULCIMERS

You don't know the Ozarks until you've heard dulcimer music. This Celtic transplant to the Ozarks via the Appalachians is a bedrock element of the region. This isn't just a music shop—it's a place for inspiration and education about the dulcimer, a historic mountain instrument, and its relatives. Dozens of fretted and hammered dulcimers are on display and ready to play, along with ukuleles, guitars, violins, and folk harps. Troy and the gang at Cedar Creek encourage everyone to play their handcrafted models, and there are many other instruments available, too. If you are more into music appreciation, don't miss the selection of CDs featuring folk music and old-time instruments.

I stop in every chance I get just to be reminded of the simple joys of music and that anyone can play an instrument—especially with the shop's proven "play by number" system. It's a great local store with friendly staff who never pressure sales. Try your hand at playing a tune and getting some of the mountain music in your soul.

3010 W. 76 Country Blvd., Branson
417-334-1395
cedarcreekdulcimers.com

FUDGE A LITTLE
AT THE FUDGE SHOP

No trip is complete without a little sweet to take home. For almost thirty years, the Fudge Shop has been treating downtown visitors with its delicious fudge, chocolate, divinity, peanut brittle, and candy. The corner store in historic Branson is a local landmark—you'll find it under the red awnings.

Ask about the "foot of chocolate" specials, and be sure to sample some of the clusters with local walnuts.

Don't forget to bring a sense of humor and some cash, because the shop does not accept debit or credit cards.

106 S. Second St., Branson
417-334-5270
facebook.com/pages/The-Fudge-Shop/140642869306185

FIND AN OUTLET
FOR YOUR MONEY

Branson boasts a lot of great shopping, but for the budget-conscious there is no better bargain than what an outlet store can provide. Fortunately for you, we have two outlet malls, and they offer different choices.

Tanger Outlets has big-name brands such as Reebok, Nike, Ann Taylor, Old Navy, Gap, Clark's, and Van Heusen. It is built in a horseshoe design, so you can start at one end and work your way to the other, stopping for an old-fashioned root beer float at A&W along the way.

The Shoppes at Branson Meadows has Tuesday Morning, ToolsUSA, Corning Factory Store, VF Outlet, and the Kitchen Collection sprinkled in a semi-circle that surrounds a central clock tower. It also boasts an eleven-screen movie theater, which runs current films as both matinee and evening shows every day.

Watch the brochures in the racks around town for current coupons and savings.

300 Tanger Blvd., Branson
800-407-2762, tangeroutlet.com/branson

The Shoppes at Branson Meadows
4562 N. Gretna Rd., Branson
417-339-2580, theshoppesatbransonmeadows.com

GET STEEPED IN NOSTALGIA
AT DICK'S 5 & 10

For fans of yesteryear, there is no better place to revel in the past than at Dick's 5 & 10. While you won't find much at fifty-year-old prices, what you will find is a smile and a memory. Toys, games, hobby supplies, sewing notions, glassware, candy, books, and memorabilia will have you twisting your way through the aisles to the oldies tunes playing from the jukebox. Its location in historic downtown Branson has been a magnet for young and old for decades. You'll know you've arrived when you see the bright red and white window displays and notice the old-fashioned variety store stock spilling out the doors. There's usually sufficient parking on the street or just behind the building in the public parking lot.

Going to the five and dime isn't just a shopping trip—it's a blast from the past.

103 W. Main St., Branson
417-334-2410
dicks5and10.com

GET A BEAD ON FASHION
AT PLUM BAZAAR

You can't miss the big purple building at the bottom of Main Street in downtown Branson. And if the color didn't give it away, these folks are serious about getting creative. Jewelry and accessory enthusiasts will be enraptured with what Plum Bazaar, filled to bursting with beads of every size, shape, and color, has to offer. Don't care to craft your own one-of-a-kind creation? Pick up a unique piece of art made by one of the shop workers. The selections are stunning!

123 E. Main St., Branson
417-337-7586
facebook.com/PlumBazaar

STITCH IT UP
AT QUILTS AND QUILTS

You might guess from the store name that it has quilts for sale. What you can't guess is that it also houses thousands of bolts of fabric and hundreds of kits for crafters to take home to begin creating their own masterpiece. For years, this prodigious fabric store was at home on the Strip, but after a devastating tornado the owners and staff refused to be beaten. They found a new location and are now bigger than ever. Near the Amish Country Store and the Branson Mill Craft Village, this is an important stop for those who want a custom-made souvenir to remember their trip.

Three generations and a combined total of two hundred years of experience make this an unforgettable visit for the seamstress or quilter. It's like a mini quilt show and fabric fair rolled into one.

3500 N. Gretna Rd., Branson
417-334-3243
quiltsandquilts.com

GET THIS LIMITED-TIME OFFER
AT AS SEEN ON TV

The As Seen On TV store is one of those bizarrely attractive places you know you shouldn't visit, but you do anyway. Products from every late-night infomercial selling the latest invention (even the Sham-Wow!) can be found within these walls. There are some surprising inventions that might just make your life better, and you'll get more than a few chuckles. It doesn't cost anything to browse, but I'm betting you'll find something irresistible to take back home. Just consider it one of those guilty pleasures you indulge in when on vacation. We'll never tell!

1219 Branson Landing Blvd., Branson
417-239-0050

SUGGESTED
ITINERARIES

HIT THE WATER

Float Your Cares Away in a Kayak, 55

Honk a Wacky Quacker on Ride the Ducks, 46

Sing, Dance, and Dine on the *Showboat Branson Belle*, 48

Visit Moonshine Beach, 78

Make a Splash at a Water Park, 79

SEE A SHOW

See a Show under the Stars at Shepherd of the
  Hills Outdoor Drama, 36

Make Legendary Memories at Legends in Concert, 39

Get Spit At by a Llama at Sight and Sound Theatres, 40

Sing, Dance, and Dine on the *Showboat Branson Belle*, 48

Thank Your Dentist at the Presleys' and Baldknobber Shows, 47

GO ON AN ADVENTURE

Wheel It or Go on the Fly at Dogwood Canyon, 54

Go Underground at Marvel Cave, 56

Go Looking for Bigfoot, 64

Go Up, Up, and Away in a Steampunk Balloon, 88

Ride the Rails with Branson Scenic Railway, 110

PUB AND WINE CRAWL

GET CREATIVE

MUSEUM JUNKIE

FAMILY FUN

FREE STUFF

See Fire and Water Unite at the Branson
Landing Fountain Show, 32

Be a Singing Sensation at Karaoke Night, 35

Sample Old-Fashioned Treats at College of the Ozarks, 98

See How a River Became a Lake at Table Rock Dam, 108

Walk the Trails of an Ozark Mountain, 72

Feed the Fish at Shepherd of the Hills Fish Hatchery, 84

Take a Ride on Sparky the Downtown Trolley, 90

SEASONAL
ACTIVITIES

SPRING

SUMMER

FALL

WINTER

INDEX